ALAMO

A Brief History of Texas including Battle of the Alamo and its Key Figures

HISTORY ENCOUNTERS

HISTORY ENCOUNTERS

Alamo

A Brief History of Texas including Battle of the Alamo and its Key Figures

Contents

Chapter One: Introduction — 1

Chapter Two: Texas Discovered — 4

Chapter Three: Spain and France's claim on Texas — 8

Chapter Four: The Battle of Republicans Versus the Spaniards... — 11

Chapter Five: The Second Attempt — 15

Chapter Six: The End of Spanish Domination — 18

Chapter Seven: The Different Missions — 20

Chapter Eight: Alamo Mission — 22

Chapter Nine: The Start — 24

Chapter Ten: The Rise to the Battle of the Alamo — 27

Chapter Eleven: The Final Battle — 29

Chapter Twelve: The Men Who Defended Texas — 33

Chapter Thirteen: Antonio Lopez de Santa Anna: A Man of... — 40

Discussion Questions 1 — 43

Discussion Questions 2 — 44

Discussion Questions 3 — 45

Discussion Questions 4 — 46

Discussion Questions 5 — 47

Discussion Questions 6 — 48

Discussion Questions 7 — 49

Discussion Questions 8 — 50

True or False Questions — 51

QUIZ ANSWER 53
Conclusion 54

Chapter One: Introduction

"I am determined to sustain myself as long as possible & die like a soldier who never forgets what is due to his own honor & that of his country." – William Travis

This quote is from a letter William Travis wrote for the people of America, specifically the people of Texas. What happened in the Alamo was tragic but inspirational. It just goes to show that victories in history are not the only ones that can impact people's stories. The losses in history are just as consequential and influential as the victories. The Battle of the Alamo expresses just that.

France was the first to discover Texan land, specifically by a named Robert Cavalier, a Sieur de la Salle, meaning he is a man who explores uncharted, undiscovered lands. Cavalier discovered Texas back in 1685, although this was not the first time he stepped foot on Texas. He came to Texas but left to get financial support from his king. He came back with the support he needed. From then on, he claimed Texas in the name of France.

Texas' history is much like many other countries. There were two countries that were fighting over the Texan land. One of them was Spain, and the other was France. That went on for a few years before the French lost. However, that was not the end of the battle over Texas. There was another battle for their land, and that battle was between the Republicans and the Spaniards. It was a long battle, and there was not only one long battle but different battles consecutively. In the end, the Mexicans defeated the Spaniards, ending the Spanish Domination of Texas.

The Battle of the Alamo, which started in December of 1835, was also known as the War for Texan Independence. The two main parties against each other in this battle were the Mexicans and the Americans. The battle was intense, and many soldiers died on both sides. And this battle was not a victorious one, at least not for the Americans. The Mexicans won this war; however, the war was nothing short of inspirational. Yes, it was a defeat, but it lit a fire in the Texan people to continue fighting for their independence, and eventually, they did win their independence from the Mexicans.

Plenty of men gave their lives for the Independence of Texas during the Battle of the Alamo. In this reading, though, we will be focusing on William Barret Travis, James Fannin, James

Bowie, and Davy Crockett. All of them were integral cogs in the machinery of the military that led against the Mexicans. The reading will also talk about Antonio Lopez de Santa Anna, a Mexican that had a major influence on the Battle of the Alamo. He was a Mexican who led the fight against the Americans who were fighting for their Texan Independence.

This reading will educate you on what happened before and during the Battle of the Alamo. You will learn the reasons behind the Battle and the people that created a difference in that historic event. You will also learn more history than you might expect, and you might think it should not be discussed. But everything is connected, no matter how far in history it is. It will still teach you a lesson and allow you to realize the reasons or motives of the people at that time.

But do not only look for the facts; learn to read through the words. Figure out what lessons you can gain from reading about the Alamo battle. Because is that not what history is all about? Is history not all about learning from the past to make way for a better and more beautiful future?

Now enough of the preparation, time for you to read about the Alamo Battle. But of course, you must learn a little bit more of the history of Texas before the Battle to fully understand the lesson.

Chapter Two: Texas Discovered

A Picture of the Alamo Church

The story of the Alamo is one of the darkest parts of Texas' history. It was more significant than the American Civil War and the war between the North and the South. Sadly, however, the story of the Alamo is not as told as the two previous wars mentioned. The detail of their struggle for independence which was brought forth by the commonwealths' power over them, is a bit hazy. The implementation of the different principles was the same as the policies put on the colonies of New England: impositions, extortions, and denial of self-government.

To give a brief background, the State of Texas was discovered by a man named Robert Cavalier, a Sieur de la Salle, back in January of 1685. This was not the first time Cavalier came to America. He arrived on America's soil only to go back to France to gain the support of their king to fund his expedition: to find the mouth of the Mississippi. He failed at his mission because he was going too far south, to the Gulf of Mexico. However, he did find the Texas shores on the Island of Matagorda.

Cavalier was able to establish a fort and a colony in this new land he found. He struggled through many conflicts with the many tribes he encountered – they call them Indians. Ironically, Cavalier was not killed by the Indians he's offended by but rather by his own men. Supposedly, he was buried on the same plot of land he was killed, near the Arkansas-Louisiana-Texas state line (of course on the Texan side) on March 16, 1687. Cavalier was able to expand the Texan territory to the far east, near Mississippi. Once the news of this new expansion and discovery reached Spain and its Crown, he sent the Mexican Viceroy to push them out of the land.

The Viceroy then left to do the orders of their Spanish crown. Their first task was to determine where Cavalier's home base was, which they found out in 1686 in Fort St. Louis. However, the Frenchmen went to an unexplored land. They were unfamiliar with the terrain, territory, and what it brought. So, they set out and found themselves infected with diseases only known to the Indians.

Besides that, the Indians were vicious and were not fond of the idea of the intrusion of the French and Spanish, who were drawn to the Monclova. The Comanches, Caranchaus, and Lipans were the foremost tribes that gave the commanders of the different invaders trouble. However, where there were hostile tribes, there were also hospitable ones, such as the Cennis and Nassonites. As the La Salles and Leons settled in, they claimed the land.

During that time, the French had claimed the territory of the Louisiana Purchase. While this is happening, Spain has claimed Mexico all the way to the Mississippi border; this includes the Gulf near Mexico.

To summarize, the first time Texas was discovered, it was being fought upon by the European monarchs: Louis the Fourteenth and King Charles. However, the whole country remained unexplored and unoccupied (not proven that there was civilization), so both monarchs felt it would be best to focus on the other conquests instead of using all their resources on the Texas expedition.

The Commandant of Louisiana stayed put, guarding the needs of his ruler. In 1721, the Monarch of France finally decided to launch an expedition. The ruler of France was advised by his advisers to claim all territory all the way to the Bay of San Bernard. However, the Indians who inhabited the land did their best to push them away. Even though their forces were no match for France's numbers, they still attacked.

While this was happening to the French, the Spaniards were

slowly but surely approaching from the Mexican side. The Franciscan monks received rewards for bringing Christianity to the Indians. Despite the battle, the trading market continues. The traders and pioneers would travel from Louisiana to Mexico and vice versa. This allowed a slow exploration of both the Eastern and Western Borders.

Because two Monarchs were fighting over Mexican land, there were many conflicts between the two rulers for some years. While their homelands were at war, their two kingdoms were at war on Mexican soil. But as the fighting continued, the Spaniards started to surpass the power of the French. Because of this power imbalance, the Spaniards introduced the Mexican settlers to ports. The monks who worked near the coastline were tasked to have missions, churches, fortifications, and schools. Therefore, Indianola, Lavaca, Matagorda, San Antonio, San Jacinto, Nacogdoches, and other Mexican settlements started their Christian ways.

In 1786, France was able to settle down and stop the battle of Mexico's territory with Spain. They proposed a treaty wherein they would share the territory instead. However, Spain offered something else that irritated the French and Indian colonists in Louisiana, which led to the organization of many parties that drove Spain away from the border.

Chapter Three: Spain and France's claim on Texas

〰️

The old road of San Antonio has been occupied by St. Denis for almost a century, according to the history written. That specific path ushered in the Nacogdoches to Monclova. Even though it was already in the late 19th century, people used this road, such as horsemen and wagoneers. Soon enough, the road expanded, moving past Louisiana and the northeast area. However, Nacogdoches was the gateway to the New Philippines. The Mission of our Lady (1715) made the first Spanish settlements that encountered other travelers, traders, and explorers looking through the undiscovered, forbidden terrain.

Towards the end of the eighteenth, the first ever white men came to Texas; that is how long ago our history says. The American army, which was stationed in Mississippi and Louisiana, was in need of new land. They sent an emissary to the

Commander at Nacogdoches to restock after what happened to the prairies a number of miles to the West. His name was Senor Commandant De Nava. The emissary they sent was named Philip Nolan, who was an American. Because of Spain's encounters with France, France was paranoid about having another government on Texan soil. It was difficult for Nolan to convince France. But he did and also got De Nava's permission. France went to Texas, setting up their own territory that was still unexplored – even the Spaniards did not explore it yet.

Nolan's first journey was all about restocking and securing a number of Mustangs without spending anything monetarily, with the exemption of the original outfitting and the cost of the peace offerings he had for the redskins.

Nolan also made a second trip back in the 1800s for the same goals as the first. He started his adventure at Natchez, going all the way to Mississippi with the safety net of a permit from the Governor of Louisiana. However, unlike his first trip, this second one was his downfall. The Spaniards soon became jealous of Nolan's personable personality towards the Indians and wanted his rapport with them for themselves. De Nava, out of jealousy, ordered the arrest of Nolan. There were some Indian spies who found out about Nolan's predicament and defended him. In the end, Nolan went away from the American army and became his own boss.

While this was happening, the colonists of Louisiana had a little game amongst themselves. They found themselves reluctant subjects of Spain, and they wanted to avenge the death of Nolan and make diplomatic negotiations with the

United States. The news of their wants carried all the way to the Southwest border of the American republic to the Spanish line. So, the old boundary argument needed to be settled quickly; the Spaniards claimed everything included in Mississippi. However, the United States trusted that their purchase encompassed everything starting from the West of Rio Grande.

However, the easternmost Spanish mission and settlement were still in Nacogdoches while the French had given the United States her West territory for the purposes of trading posts and fortification; these lands are Natchitoches and Sabine. The lake stream became the temporary boundary line; it separated the two forces, and crossing the stream meant war.

The Mexican governor repositioned his headquarters from San Antonio to Nacogdoches. At the same time, the American Commander moved to the front of New Orleans. However, they all wanted to win through diplomacy, and the Spaniards did just that. Because of this, the American forces were banned from the land.

Chapter Four: The Battle of Republicans Versus the Spaniards for Texas

An artwork about the Battle of the Alamo

With no significant boundary lines, Texas could break Spain's hold on their land. Nolan was able to make a loyal protégée before his death. This American lieutenant's name is Augustus Magee. During the war of 1812, he gained visibility when he decided to stage a coup in Texas to make the land an independent republic. A former Mexican revolutionist assisted him with this plan.

They were able to bring together the very first independent invading group that's purpose was to bring down Spain. The group was filled with adventurers who stayed near the neutral grounds of Nacogdoches; they were unhappy with Spanish soldiers. Part of the group is also Mexicans and Indian people. They stand together with a number of dismissed soldiers and trustworthy Americans.

Their first attack was through the American lines. Even though it began as a neutral strip of land and was mainly populated by Americans, the attack was to capture the fort of Nacogdoches; the Spaniards offered no resistance because they ran away towards the West to San Antonio the moment their eyes landed on the invaders.

Gutierrez was a defeated Mexican revolutionist who was in command when Magee fled to New Orleans to get more funds for the upcoming war. When Magee came back from New Orleans, he had come back with funds and recruits who were willing to join forces with Gutierrez on the Trinity, a merged army of republican struggles and adventurers from the St. Denis Road. They captured Goliad and absorbed the Spanish garrison into their ranks, making their troops much stronger.

Kemper, an American, took the place of Magee after everything. He was able to survive all of the Spaniards' attacks until they finally gave up their siege on them and just strengthened and focused more on their missions.

Gutierrez and Kemper were in a battle for a long time. They fought from nine miles from the city of Rosillo. The Spanish armies outnumbered the Republicans greatly, which was a big challenge the Republicans took up. This battle for them was important because if they had lost, their cause would have been for nothing. If they had won, they would have had the chance of taking Texas and making a great city out of it, with respect to the Indians.

The battle of Rosillo Creek affected the fate of San Antonio City. This city gave up its freedom at the sight of the Americans. However, seventeen Spaniards fought them as they guarded the Church and the Fortress of Alamo. This is connected to the battle of Rosillo because it turned into a slaughter of the surrendered and captured Republican officers. Gutierrez declared that the surrendered men would be freed; however, they were followed by parole officers while the men who fought back were executed brutally. This cruel event created a domino effect, influencing the determination of the American residents at the Alamo to fight back.

This brutality was because of the Mexican orders and not from the American commander. However, they were all still considered Republicans. Even though they were losing, the Spaniards were not falling back, at least not under the command of Elizondo. The attack on San Antonio happened on June 4, 1813. During this battle, the Republican forces were protected by the fortifications that were made. They won this battle because of their defenses, and for a time, that was enough for the Republicans/Mexicans. But it wasn't going to last. The tides turned after two months, in the month of August.

Kemper went back to Nacogdoches after the battle of Rosillo. He did not want to go back while Gutierrez was in the picture because he was responsible for the deaths of Governors Salcedo, Herrera, and Cordero. A number of the best American officers resigned and followed Kemper and soon after made sure that Gutierrez gave up his power to General Toledo, who decided to return to Nacogdoches to recruit more people for his troop and get more funds to help support them in the war. However, General Arredondo came to Mexico to replace Elizondo. Because of this, Toledo did not stay safe in the defenses of the Alamo. Instead, he decided to fight.

Then came a vast war, and the Republican army was annihilated; they were no match against their opponents. Only 93 Americans escaped, and that count already includes the Mexicans, half-breed French people, and Indian people. They made their way back to Nacogdoches, and the very first war for Texas independence came to a sad end.

Chapter Five: The Second Attempt

A plaque of Travis' Letter to the Texan People

After five years during the battle of the Medina, a Tennessean named Dr. James Long, a man who served under General Jackson at New Orleans, had become inspired to immortalize himself through the independence of Texas. He also wants to give a hand in creating a foundation of a small American republic with an invasion at Natchez. He led his army to Nacogdoches to shift the war in their favor.

Because of his goals, General Long created a "Republic of Texas" at Nacogdoches and was successful in making the republic annexed to the United States. However, even though Long organized this system of government, he was not finished. Eventually, he did establish a legislature that helped make and apply the revenue and immigration laws. Although his attempts succeeded, it was a short run – his success lasted only for only 25 years.

Eventually, the Spaniards demolished Long's established government because he was not there to defend it. He was trying to recruit Lafitte, a Frenchman, to ask for his help against his struggle with the Mexicans.

Lafitte was a Frenchman from New Orleans who helped found the island of Galveston. He was able to organize the colony of that land. He allowed a number of men (both French and Indian) to accumulate their own wealth by using privateering the Spanish vessels that roamed the Gulf.

Lafitte had his own opinions on the republic of Texas. However, he decided not to join Long in his mission. The whole of Mexico then chose to overthrow the Spanish governor; they took advantage of the fact that Spain was all the way to the other side of the sea, meaning their hold on the Mexican colonies would not be as strong due to the distance.

Lafitte was cunning. Both Magee and Long's adventures and goals failed because of the numbers in their belt. Also, Magee's and Long's plans were too early – they were not planned properly. Long tried his luck again in 1821, and he was able to go so far as to the West as Goliad, then all the way to La Bahia. However, he only had 52 men in his army, and then they were overpowered by the Mexican force.

Chapter Six: The End of Spanish Domination

A picture of James Bowie

The decline of the Spanish rule in Texas was because of Moses Austin and his introduction of colonists in Texas back in 1820. Austin came from Missouri, and he was a pioneer of proclivities. He succeeded in gathering a permit to occupy a selected spot of land with his men. However, they had to run with the demands of the Spaniards. They had to have good character, swear allegiance to Spain, must be Roman Catholics, be able not to pay taxes for six years, give men to their workforce, and so on. However, before he could perfect their contract, Austin died. His son, Stephen F. Austin, who was 28 years old, took up his father's work and was able to introduce the colony by the winter of 1821.

They barely had any time to introduce the newcomers and orient them to their work on the farm when Mexico started a revolt against Spain and started a war on the Mexica peninsula. The Spanish governor of San Antonio was not able to stick to the terms of the contract, letting Stephen Austin go to the City of Mexico to negotiate the terms for the future of his people.

After two years, Stephen Austin got permission to bring almost 500 more families into his colony. He was also able to give small grants to the settlement of Texas. Hayden Edwards, from Kentucky, was given a grant that created minor chaos. There was a constant fight between the Colonists and the Mexicans on the ownership of land, water, rights, timber, etc. In the end, while Edwards was not present, another colony led by a Mexica governor annulled the grant given to him. It forced the leaders out of the country. There was resistance to this order, and the men called themselves "Fredonians." Still, they were unsuccessful, so they returned to Louisiana.

Eventually, Mexico defeated Spain, which became an independent country and government.

Chapter Seven: The Different Missions

This is a list that summarizes the many missions made by the Spaniards to find new land and claim it as their territory:

- St. John the Baptist on the Rio Grande, which is where Laredo stood in 1690.
- Our Lady of Guadalupe at Victoria in 1714
- Mission Orquizacas on the San Jacinto River in 1715
- Mission Dolores near San Augustine in 1716
- Our Lady of Nacogdoches in 1715
- Mission Adaes, East of the Sabine River in 1718
- Mission Espiritu Santo, at Goliad then Bahia 1718
- Mission San Jose, San Antonio 1718
- Mission de la Conception 1731
- Mission San Juan de Capistrano 1731
- Mission San Fernando 1731

- Mission San Francisco de la Espada 1731

And the mission this whole reading is about: The Alamo on the Rio Grande in 1703, removed to San Antonio in 1718 on to the spot where it stood in 1722. You would see that the Spaniards have not stopped looking for different and important places for the other Spaniards to have. We have reason to believe that the work that was mapped out in the second decade of the then century was good enough to keep the government and the church civil.

When it was the middle to the latter part of the eighteenth century, there were missions wherein they must create an association for Indian schools. The reason for these missions is that it tracks the schooling of the same general character as them. The Alamo Mission was one of these missions. There were special architects about the Franciscans gathered together to make a plan wherein the whole Western Louisiana line could be connected to Mexico. Their plan was to have a good effect on the salutatory of the Indians and satisfy the Spanish and Canary Island colonists; these two groups of people founded elegant churches, homes, beautiful catholic schools, and well-grounded trading posts. Sadly, so many historical events have not been fully documented during this time.

Chapter Eight: Alamo Mission

In the 18th century, a Franciscan mission entitled "Alamo" happened in Texas. It has become a place that showed the historical resistance of a small group of Texan fighters who fought for their state's independence from Mexico.

The Texas Revolution started in December 1835, also known as the War of Texan Independence. It started the way all wars began, a forced occupation of a land that its current people would not have accepted willingly. In the Texan War, Mexican forces from San Antonio followed through with their occupation of the Alamo. There were some Texan leaders, such as Sam Houston, who was the Commanding General of the Texas Army, who suggested leaving San Antonio since it seemed almost impossible to protect and save. However, that did not stop a group of brave men from the Alamo who refused to back down.

February 23, 1863, a roughly 1,800 men army from Mexico,

who was commanded by General Antonio Lopez de Santa Anna, came from the south by the Rio Grande. From there, they all rushed to gain complete control of the Alamo. Even with the fierce fight the Texans had within them; they did not win this battle. However, this battle at the Alamo became a symbol of Texan resistance in the state. The battle of San Jacinto happened on April 21, 1836. During this battle, the Texans screamed, "Remember Alamo!" as their battle cry.

Chapter Nine: The Start

The struggle to grab independence for Texas started with Gonzales on the first of October. A town owned a cannon that was given by the government four years ago when they needed it to defend themselves from the Indians. Due to a Mexican Colonel who wanted to disable and get the gun from them, a battle started. The people did not want to give up their weapons so quickly, so they used them against the Colonel and his men. They retreated and succeeded in escaping; however, there were casualties.

The next big fight was at Goliad. This is where a group of Texans, estimated at fifty to sixty in number, who are mostly factory workers, went to battle under the command of Colonel Ben Milam. They captured the garrison with hundreds of people, and they were able to acquire a number of cannons and a supply of ammunition and military stores. This movement of theirs was spreading; they were dead set on fighting for justice and their independence.

However, the Mexicans, who were their allies against the Spaniards, were not sitting back and relaxing. Santa Anna sent General Cos, his own brother-in-law, who is also one of the best commanders of the Mexican army, to lead the charge at San Antonio. Reinforcements arrived at the garrison, which solidified the fortifications. The Mexicans also prepared for the battle.

Austin was prepared. He knew that it was a need to have supplies that reached the West. His council, who went with him westward, included Houston, Bowie, Travis, Fannin, Crockett, Milam, Burleson, and Deaf Smith. This left Gonzales with only 350 men, which is not precisely a large army, but it was a passionate army. They won't let anything get in their way. By the time he arrived at the Mission of de la Espada (also known as the Mission of the Sword and the Fourth Mission at San Antonio), his numbers increased to beyond 600 men who were hell-bent on setting Texas free.

Austin deployed some couriers from la Espada to San Antonio with the command to make General Cos surrender. However, the couriers were met with negativity. Their ties were destroyed, and the opposing commanders challenged them by throwing the gauntlet to the ground.

Austin and his council took just a few minutes to decide their next step. On the morning of the twenty-seventh of October, Fannin and Bowie were deployed along with a hundred or so men to have their first mission: Mission of the Immaculate Concepcion, which was two miles south of the Alamo, which was the main fortress and headquarters of the Mexican people.

During the first mission, San Antonio started a skirmish with the Mexicans as aggressors. General Cos deployed an army to make Fannin and Bowie retreat, so they attacked them on the 28th at sunrise. The army that attacked consisted of a troop of cavalry and a battalion of artillery. However, the Americans were not at all helpless. They knew their way around a rifle, and the Mexicans were not prepared for their skill. After the attack, the Mexicans were forced to retreat; before they could regroup under cover of their weapons, they lost their first Mexican hero to the War for Independence.

After that day, other skirmishes happened in that city, and it went on across the month to November. General Edward Burleson was the successor of Austin. He kept his forces close to him; he was patient, waiting for reinforcements before attacking the Alamo. However, the colonists were not as patient as he was, so his army became restless.

After such a long time, Colonel Milam led a troop of volunteers, around the numbers of 300, for a number of days to the West side of the river; this ran down to Soledad Street to the now-current Santa Rosa Hospital and City Market House. Milam and his men slaughtered the court of the old Veramendi House. Colonel Johnson took his place after Milam, and the fight continued for several days. Finally, on the ninth of December, the Alamo surrendered and became the property of the American colonists.

Chapter Ten: The Rise to the Battle of the Alamo

After the American colonists' occupation of Alamo, several events happened. The Convention of Consultation appointed a provisional government even though they chose not to withdraw from Mexico and, at the same time, set up a republic. They were competent enough to set up a home rule and enforce restrictive and unfair laws. However, this did not satisfy the extremists of the patriots. This caused them to have random outbursts led by the republicans,

Henry Smith was then appointed as provisional governor, and General Sam Houston was elected the Commander-in-Chief of the American armies. While Austin, Archer, and Wharton were made to go to Washington to be part of the board of commissioners for Texas. They thought this was smart because it would show the people, through diplomacy, that they were here for peace. Although, it did not make much difference because the revolt had become too broad.

He took command of the different armies when the Mexicans started elaborately preparing for their subsequent invasion to ensure their power stayed where it was (their dictatorship in Texas). He combined them to bring them to San Antonio.

Chapter Eleven: The Final Battle

An artwork of the Battle of the Alamo

The Mexican troops set up camp in the Medina. Then they deployed men in advance to spy on the American encampment to find out their numbers and get any other critical information that may help them win this fight. They found that the Americans' encampment wasn't as well established as theirs. Hence, the Mexicans pressed forward to the Alazan, which was three miles west of the town of the

Alamo.

Since there was no way to communicate with the frontier, they were not prepared for the opposing side. They expected reinforcements during their initial march to the West; however, they were growing impatient because of the leaders and council's contentions. Their decision caused a delay in their march to the Alamo. Eventually, the Mexican army planned to come during the night to be hidden by the shadows. By the sunrise of February 23, they were found circling the prairies West of the San Pedro and lining through the banks of Alazan.

An alarm went off by the sentinel tower, which produced the biggest consternation in the history of this city. Dr. Sutherland and Smith volunteered to be sent to gather information on whether the alarm was an actual event or a fake one. They discovered that just west of San Pedro, there was an army. As the sun was about to rise, they knew they had to fight.

The mission still continued, and where that went, death followed. With their brave men, Travis and Bowie were already aware of their defenses crumbling lest some reinforcements come their way. However, they have yet to receive any. So, within the town of Alamo, the provisions of their fortress have been depleted.

All Americans hid behind the fort except for one: Dr. Sutherland. He deployed himself to the command center in San Felipe to request reinforcements. However, the place is too far away. During his absence, the men by the frontiers suffered at Goliad and Medina compared to the war battles in other colonies. Dr.

Sutherland's efforts, however gallant they were, were fruitless because he did not even reach San Felipe.

The gates of the Alamo were barely barricaded when the messengers of Santa Anna came and demanded their immediate surrender. Travis did not like the idea, so he fired a shot from the cannon on the roof of the fortress to intimidate the enemy. He also waved their blood-red flag around, and the people of the Alamo saw it and already got his message: it was time to fight.

Travis was in command of this battle, with Bowie as his right-hand man. Crockett, who was originally in Tennessee after he lost the re-election of his position in the American Congress, was given command by Travis. However, he declined Travis' offer.

Davy Crockett was a Tennessee frontiersman who the people of Texas are proud to call their own. He led his people through the fight with the Indians and outlaws who were hostile then – he did not stop until there was peace in the land. However, he had no plans of being the leader of the Texans. But he did, and he led the revolution that gave them the Liberty of the Lone Star Republic.

As the Mexicans closed in on the Alamo by dawn, all of them were equipped with battle gear, their forces in many numbers. On the side of the Alamo, General Cos, who the Americans highly view, led his men of Montezumas to the Eats walls. Santa Anna came from the other side of the river, which was behind the leading troop of the army. The Mexicans pressed on to battle, coming closer and closer to the town's lines, but Travis, Crockett, and Bonham did not show any fear.

After many excruciating days, the battle is upon them. The Mexican army went on and attacked the outer walls with their artillery until it all came crumbling down. The people of Texas fought with all they had. However, it wasn't enough. The numbers advantage is something that the Texans did not have. It was a gory battle with many casualties, mainly on the side of the Texans.

By the time it was mid-afternoon, the battle had ended, and the Americans had won. They finally achieved their goal of occupying the Alamo; however, the Americans' win came at a price: many people died in this battle – on both sides. But the rewards for the Americans were great. About 176 Americans held their own for the twelve days – or instead, until they massacred each and every enemy.

The siege and battle of the Alamo stirred excitement in the country's people and piqued the United States' interest due to Texas. Individually, the citizens of Texas took a stand and commemorated the heroes of their war in hopes that they would be free again.

Chapter Twelve: The Men Who Defended Texas

A Statue of William Travis

William Barret Travis

William Barret Travis was a commander back in the battle of the Alamo. Travis came to Texas early in 1831 because the Law made his immigration illegal on April 6, 1839. On May 21, he was given land by Stephen F. Austin. He set up his legal practice in Anahuac, which was an essential port of entry stationed on the eastern end of Galveston Bay. He traveled across the country doing legal work and acquainting himself with some military groups who were against the Law of April 6, 1830. Soon enough, the group he met and is now a part of was known as the war party, created due to the growing tension between the Mexican government versus the American people of Texas. Travis had multiple opportunities to go against the commander of the Mexican garrison back in Anahuac, whose name was Colonel John Davis Bradburn. This commander helped implement the anti-immigration Law, which inhibited the state officials from isolating and giving the land to American settlers.

After what happened in Anahuac in 1832, Travis relocated his legal practice from Anahuac to San Felipe. After two years, Travis was appointed secretary to the ayuntamiento; he was then part of the councils of government. After Stephen F. Austin brought up his petition of the Convention of 1833 to the government of Mexico City, he was incarcerated up until the year 1835. At this point, Antonio Lopez de Santa Anna had fully asserted himself to the Centralist authority. She rebuilt a custom house and military group at Anahuac with the help of Captain Antonio Tenorio. James B. Miller, with the authorization of Travis, led a group of fighters to go back to Anahuac to expel Tenorio. By late June, Travis led a group of 25 men through Harrisburg, passing Galveston Bay, to bring on an assault to Tenorio; with his small group of men, he easily captured the Mexican soldiers in that area. Because this act was alarming to the peace party, many saw Travis as a person who must be looked out for. General Martin Perfecto de Cos, a Mexican military Commander, regarded Travis and other people on his side as Anahuac outlaws who he demanded to surrender to a military trial.

However, when Cos demanded the immediate surrender of Gonzales back in October 1835, Travis and a few hungry Texans tried to support Gonzales, but they were too late. Travis later prepared the San Antonio de Valero Mission (known now as the Alamo Mission) for the Mexican Army. With the help of Green B. Jameson, an engineer, they could set up good defenses. However, it was not enough. The Mexicans quickly overtook the Texans in only a few hours.

Travis died early on in the battle; his body, along with the other dead Texan men, was burned. Travis' death was a catalyst for his being seen as not just a commander but a true hero of Texas.

James Fannin

James Walker Fannin, Jr. was an activist for the Texas Revolution. On August 20, 1835, the Committee of Safety and Correspondence of Columbia chose to use his influence on his people for a consultation. On August 27, Fannin asked the United States Army in Georgia to supply financial aid for the Texas cause and bring in officers for the Texan army. Fannin, in September, was an active member of the volunteer army and gave money to the expedition to capture the Veracruzana, which was a Mexican ship at Copano. On October 6 of the same year, he was part of a committee that agreed with Stephen F. Austin's plan to aid Gonzales.

Fannin was ordered to sabotage the Mexican supply route that goes from Laredo to San Antonio; however, he was not supported in this attempt. On November 13, the commander-in-chief, Sam Houston, offered Fannin the position of Inspector General. He also got an honorable discharge from the volunteer army, so Fannin had time to join the regular army. The General Council, in December, finally taking Fannin's advice, made an auxiliary volunteer corps. Houston made Fannin the Colonel of the regular army by December 7. By December 10, the council demanded his name to be part of the reinforcements.

As he continued his life as an agent of the provisional government, Fannin, by January of the following year, started recruiting people to be a part of the Matamoros expedition. After Houston backed out of the said expedition, Fannin was appointed as the Colonel of the Provisional Regiment of Volunteers at Goliad and soon became the army's commander-in-chief. When he figured out that the Mexicans, under the leadership of Jose de Urrea, conquered Matamoros, Fannin immediately demanded a fallback to add more strength to the defenses at Goliad.

Fannin deployed most of his men to aid the Texans who were stationed at Refugio. He was about to call for a retreat back on March 19. However, it was too late, and they were surrounded and made to surrender at the battle of Coleto. The Texans were imprisoned at Goliad and then murdered because of Antonio

Lopez de Santa Anna's ruling, this included Fannin.

James Bowie

James Bowie, fondly known as Jim Bowie, is a known hero of the Texan Revolution because of his contribution to the Battle of the Alamo. Bowie and his parents migrated to Missouri first before going to Louisiana. Then he left home at the age of 18 and was said to have been involved in the slave trade for a while with his two brothers, John and Rezin. Then he was able to bring an improvement to the Louisiana sugar plantation; he also served in the state legislature of Louisiana and immersed himself in the New Orleans society.

Bowie then moved to Texas in 1828, during which he created a good rapport with the Mexican Vice Governor, Juan Martin de Veramendi. Because of this, he got his Mexican citizenship, got his own land grants, and married Veramendi's daughter, Ursula.

When he became the Texan Army Colonel, he fought with Colonel William B. Travis in many battles, including the Battle of the Alamo. Although he was ill, he still fought for the Texan Revolution. He was killed alongside many of the Alamo fighters due to the massive numbers on the side of the Mexicans.

David "Davy" Crockett

Crockett started his military career in September 1813; he enlisted in the militia as a scout under the command of Major Gibson in Winchester, Tennessee. He did this to avenge an Indian attack on Fort Mims, Alabama. By New Year's Day of 1821, the turning point of his military career came. He sent in his resignation to run for a political seat in the Tennessee legislature as a representative of Lawrence and Hickman counties. He won, and from then, he took an active interest in the public land policy of the West. Then in 1823, he was reelected, moving further than Dr. William E. Butler but later on, he lost in August 1825 as he tried to be part of the Congress. When he moved to Memphis, Maj M. B. Winchester encouraged him to run for Congress again, and he won against General William Arnold and Colonel Adam Alexander in 1827. He was again reelected in 1829. After that, his reputation as a sharpshooter, hunter, and yarn spinner became known. He became the model for Nimrod Wildfire and the hero of James Kirke Paulding's play "The Lion of the West." There was a book based on his life entitled "Life and Adventures of Colonel David Crockett of West Tennessee." Which was published back in 1833.

With some momentum, Crockett defeated Fitzgerald in the run to be part of Congress yet again in 1833. The next year, he was able to publish an autobiography with the help of Thomas Chilton. Obviously, Crockett saw himself as a force to be reckoned with. Because he was sure that the political process from his former constituents was not good enough, Crockett decided to help Texas. He wrote about his departure so that he could explore Texas and return. At this point, he was unaware he would be part of the fight for Texas Independence.

When William, Patton, Abner Burgin, Lindsey K. Tinkle, and David Crockett reached Memphis, they all went to Union Hotel's bar to have a farewell drinking party. Then the next day, they left – their route included passing by Arkansas, all the way to the Red River, which was along the northern boundary of Texas, then across that very river to Clarksville, to Nacogdoches and San Augustine, and off to San Antonio. When they arrived at San Augustine, the party separated ways. Burgin and Tinkle returned home while Crockett and Patton made a formal allegiance and continued to Texas.

By early February, Crockett arrived at San Antonio de Bexar, while Antonio Lopez de Santa Anna came on February 23. The Americans in Texas were divided into two political factions, and Crockett joined the faction of Colonel William B. Travis, who chose to disregard Sam Houston's orders to retreat from the Alamo battle. Crockett lost his life during the Battle of the Alamo on March 6, 1836.

Chapter Thirteen: Antonio Lopez de Santa Anna: A Man of Mexico

A painting of Antonio Lopez de Santa Anna

Antonio Lopez de Santa Anna de Lebron was a soldier and was the President of Mexico for five consecutive terms. Santa Anna was born in Jalapa, Vera Cruz, on a cold day on February 21, 1794. His family was part of the criollo middle class; his father also served as a sub-delegate for the Spanish province of Vera Cruz.

By June 1810, he was made a cadet assigned to the Fijo de Vera Cruz infantry regiment under the leadership of Joaquin de Arredondo. He stayed there for five years, battling insurgents and controlling the Indian tribes of the Provincias Internas. Along with many criollo officers in the Royalist army, he was loyal to Spain for a significant number of years. He even fought against the movement for Mexican Independence.

By 1813, he was in Texas, battling the Gutierrez-Magee expedition; during the battle of Medina, he was known for his bravery. During the aftermath of the rebellion, someone witnessed Arredondo's firm counterinsurgency policy of mass executions, and most historians hypothesized that Santa Anna was the one behind this policy. He then continued his service under Arredondo, fighting against the filibustering expedition of Francisco Xavier Mina back in 1817.

Santa Anna devoted his next several years to building Indian villages. At the same time, he collected debts, property, and promotions from them. By 1820, he was promoted to brevet captain and soon after brevet lieutenant colonel the following year. During the month of March back in 1821, he made a drastic shift of allegiance by joining the rebel forces of Agustin de Iturbide in the middle of a battle against them. He promoted Iturbide for some time, and then he became Brigadier General. In December 1822, Santa Anna cut ties with Iturbide because of personal differences.

After he served as Military Governor of Yucatan, Santa Anna retired from his life as a soldier. She climbed the political ladder, starting out as the governor of Vera Cruz. In 1829, he thwarted the Spanish Invasion at Tampico and became a national hero. He used his military experience to help him govern during his time as governor. He also went against the administration for three years before being appointed the President of Mexico as a liberal in 1833; however, in 1834, he observed that Mexico was not ready to be a democracy, so he shifted the political system to become an Autocratic Centralist.

Some liberals did not like his decision, so they tried to reduce the militia numbers in 1835; however, Santa Anna successfully defeated them. In December of 1835, he came to San Luis Potosi to organize an invasion to stop the rebellion in Texas. By 1836, he moved forward with his plan, coming from the north. After he crushed the army of Sam Houston, he was asked to go to Washington, D.C., then back to Mexico. After that, he retired to his land at Manga de Clavo but came back and joined the defenses of Mexico against the French during the "Pastry War" in December of 1838. He may have lost a leg in battle, but he still regained his popularity. He was the President in 1839, and during that year, he helped overthrow the Anastasio Bustamante Government in 1841. He turned into a dictator in 1841–1845, and that quickly turned into a mess since he was overthrown and exiled to Havana.

Discussion Questions 1

Texas has such a rich history, like all countries. But, like all history, it is still special. In your opinion, what about the discovery of Texas makes it different from the other countries?

Discussion Questions 2

Texas has struggled to win its independence for many years. At first, their land was a battleground for different parties trying to win Texas land for their own civilizations. Why do you think it took the Texan people around two rounds of different parties fighting on their land to finally fight for their own land finally?

Discussion Questions 3

The battle at the Alamo wasn't a success story but was still an inspiration for the Texans to continue their battle for independence. At one point, they even made it their battle cry. Why do you think such a defeat sparked a fire in them?

Discussion Questions 4

Battles can never always be a success. The Battle of the Alamo is one example. What do you think is the reason behind the failure of that battle?

Discussion Questions 5

Independence is something we all strive for. However, it is not something we always have. We've got to fight for it. If you were to go to battle for independence, what would you be fighting for? Independence from what?

Discussion Questions 6

Texas lost at the Battle of the Alamo, yet they never stopped fighting for their independence. That is until they got it. What about independence do you think people always strive to gain?

Discussion Questions 7

There are many people who would stop you from getting what you want. Antonio Lopez de Santa Anna was one of those people who tried to stop the Texans from getting what they wanted. Who are the people who stop you from getting what you want in your own life? Why do you think they are stopping you from achieving your goal?

Discussion Questions 8

Where there are enemies, there are always allies. In your life right now, who are your allies? Are they like Crockett, Bowie, Fannin, and Travis? What about them makes them your allies?

True or False Questions

1. *True or False.* Texas spent many years unclaimed by anyone but the Indians. The first person to discover their land was Antonio Lopez de Santa Anna. He was a Mexican man who made himself known and established a colony in Texas in the name of his country.

2. *True or False.* Texas was first occupied by France. Then the Spaniards. And right after that, the Mexicans.

3. *True or False.* There were many men who gave their lives for the Independence of Texas. Some of them were: William Travis, David Crockett, James Fannin, and David Bowie.

4. *True or False.* The Battle of the Alamo was known to be the first battle of Texan Independence. The Spaniards and the Americans were battling in this war. However, the

Americans lost the battle to the Spaniards.

5. *True or False.* The Battle of the Alamo inspired the people to continue fighting for their independence. They even made Alamo their battle cry. They all fought until they achieved their independence.

6. *True or False.* The Alamo mission started in the 18th century. It was led by a Franciscan. The year it was planned to happen and did happen was 1703.

7. *True or False.* Before the Alamo battle, the Spaniards were in control of Texas. Then the Mexicans drove them out, claiming Texas as their own. But before the Spaniards occupied Texas, it was France who had their grip on the land for many years.

8. *True or False.* Cavalier was the one who discovered Texas. However, before claiming it in the name of France, he had to go back home to request financial aid from his king. However, he was not granted financial aid, so he found his own way to get the money he needed.

QUIZ ANSWER

True or False Answers

1. False. The man who found Texas was Robert Cavalier
2. True
3. False. One of them was JAMES Bowie, not David Bowie
4. False. The Americans were against the Mexicans, not the Spaniards
5. True
6. True
7. True
8. False. The king granted him financial aid

Conclusion

This quote is not exactly exclusive to only Americans; it is for the whole world. In every war and battle fought in history, you would notice that most – if not all – civilizations would never go down without a fight. And that is something that must be praised about us humans and our nature to defend what we believe in. Yes, some beliefs are not ideal and friendly, but you should focus on this: people will fight for what they believe in, and that thinking alone should be commendable.

To connect this to the Battle of the Alamo, they may have lost. However, they did go down fighting. And not only that, but the Battle of the Alamo was also the inspiration for the subsequent wars for Texan Independence. Yes, they did not win, and it was a gruesome end. However, it served as a launch point for the subsequent battles for their independence.

Freedom is expensive and a luxury that not everyone can afford; however, it is what everyone strives to get. And yes, John F. Kennedy is correct. Everyone wants it; therefore, everyone will pay the price – and the price ranges from something as little as perhaps a plot of land to one's life. I have a question for you: is freedom really worth any risk? What makes freedom and independence have such high demand? Or do you think it is overrated?

No matter what your answer is, there will be some people who will always think freedom and independence are worth everything. And there is nothing wrong with that thinking. You will crave it if you've lived your whole life with little freedom. And that is not a terrible thing to want. Independence and freedom are two concepts all people wish for at least one point in their lives. But another question that comes up is: are you ready for it?

Going back to the Battle of the Alamo, we could not say that the Texans were not ready for independence. That is something we won't be able to see just by reading about it. But it was obvious that the Texans wanted it badly. And at first, they did not succeed, but soon enough, they did. That is another trait we should be proud to call a human trait. We do not stop until we achieve what we want. Yes, it is a bit problematic when you put it in a context, but as a trait alone, it is pretty admirable.

What you should learn from the story of the Battle of the Alamo is these two human traits: the urge to fight for what one believes in and wants and the need not to stop until you achieve your goal. If you think about it, these two traits also make us human. Animals do not have this kind of thinking, so it is a human trait. And it is something you must learn to have consciously. Not being aware of the attribute could be deadly and completely wrong. But just know that you have these traits, and remember to always use them with discretion.